Embrace Your Weirdness

OrangeBooks Publication

Smriti Nagar, Bhilai, Chhattisgarh - 490020

Website: **www.orangebooks.in**

© Copyright, 2022, Author

All rights reserved. No part of this book may be reproduced, stored in a retrieval system, or transmitted, in any form by any means, electronic, mechanical, magnetic, optical, chemical, manual, photocopying, recording, or otherwise, without the prior written consent of its writer.

First Edition, 2022
ISBN: 978-93-5621-147-6

The opinions/ contents expressed in this book are solely of the author and do not represent the opinions/ standings/ thoughts of OrangeBooks.

Embrace Your Weirdness

Why Being Weird Makes You Interesting
And Can Give You An Unfair Advantage

Mustafa Mun

OrangeBooks Publication
www.orangebooks.in

Embrace
YOUR WEIRDNESS

Why Being Weird Makes You Interesting and Can Give You an Unfair Advantage

Disclaimer

This eBook has been written for information purposes only. Every effort has been made to make this eBook as complete and accurate as possible. However, there may be mistakes in typography or content. Also, this eBook provides information only up to the publishing date. Therefore, this eBook should be used as a guide - not as the ultimate source.

The purpose of this eBook is to educate. The author and the publisher do not warrant that the information contained in this eBook is fully complete and shall not be responsible for any errors or omissions. The author and publisher shall have neither liability nor responsibility to any person or entity concerning any loss or damage caused or alleged to be caused directly or indirectly by this ebook.

This eBook offers information and is designed for educational purposes only. You should not rely on this information as a substitute, nor does it replace professional medical advice, diagnosis, or treatment.

Table of Contents

Introduction 2
- Embrace YOU 5

Who Wants To Be Normal?... 9

Being Weird Makes You Authentic 12
- Being Unique Makes You Creative.......................... 13
- You Lose a Lot When You're Not Authentic 14

Think Outside The Box With Your Weirdness........ 18
- Always Try New Things 19
- Remember Your Story is Different 19
- Tap Your Weirdness Potential 21

Embracing Your Weird Makes You
Mentally Strong 24

Weirdness Makes You Irreplaceable: The
Unfair Advantage Of Being Weird 27
- You Aren't Afraid of Speaking Your Mind 27
- You Should Never Hide Your Feelings.................... 28

- You Are Comfortable in Your Own Skin 28
- You Are Creative 29
- You Are Mentally Strong 30
- They Say No 31
- They're Adaptable 31
- They Believe in Themselves 32

Get Noticed For Your Weirdness: How To Embrace Your Weirdness 35
- Create New Skills 35
- Stay Curious 36
- Follow Your Passions 36
- Read - A LOT 36
- Be Unconventional 37

Being Weird In The Office 39
- Being Normal is Boring 41
- Being Different Makes You Noticeable 42
- Being Odd is Surprising - and Exciting 42
- Being Unique Makes You Memorable 42
- Being Normal is Easy to Imitate 43

Never Be Forgotten By Embracing Your Weirdness 45
- They're Never Boring 46

- They Always Reveal New Things............................ 46
- They Teach You About Yourself............................ 47
- They Teach you that No One is Normal................... 47

Conclusion **49**

Introduction

Introduction

Let's face it, high school is challenging. Not so much the lessons, which tend to be pretty simple. The most difficult aspect of high school is negotiating the norms and expectations of an opinionated adolescent micro-society and doing everything possible, including tremendous leaps of energy and inventiveness, to avoid doing or doing anything that would earn the unshakeable label of being odd. Being labeled as unusual in high school is a death sentence. So most people try to appear like everyone else. However, in the end, we are all hiding.

We're still figuring out who we are and where we fit on the social interaction spectrum. Mistakes are unavoidable, but they should be committed in secret, away from the limelight of the halls, lunchroom, or special events. High school students are permitted to be nervous wrecks, fearful that their own shadow would mock them if they slip and fall. However, it should have stopped there.

Shouldn't the crushing desire for peer acceptance go away after we graduate from high school and become well-adjusted adults? The high school years are long gone, yet the social pressure to adhere to others' expectations remains as powerful as it has ever been. Everyone, young and old, it seems, is still terrified of seeming odd. This widespread sense of unease overlooks a fundamental fact. It's OK to be eccentric. Weirdness is frequently a sign of latent power waiting to be unlocked.

Throughout history, the finest and brightest among us, the great inventors and innovators, have been those who have been ready to stand out and risk being viewed as strange. We are free to harness and expand the power of our various differences when I allow you to be you and you let me be me, without judgment or criticism. Nobody is normal because everyone is strange.

And it's okay to be strange! It's okay to be unique! It's okay to be different! In fact, it's natural. And, really, it's the only way to be.

Why?

Personality occurs on a continuum. There is no correct or incorrect position on the spectrum. The concept of being objectively normal was invented in order to sell things and advance political goals. What I consider to be normal may not be normal for you. We lose sight of the natural when we seek the conventional. The new normal is natural.

We all have characteristics that distinguish us from one another, whether they be physical, intellectual, emotional, or other. The Ego believes that differences are defects that should be concealed. The fact is that your superpower is what distinguishes you. You simply haven't figured out how to use it yet. Instead of concealing your oddness, figure out how to make it work for you. For example, your timidity may make you a better listener. Your uncomfortable chuckle may endear you to others. When we conquer our peculiarities, we gain immense power.

When you strive to fit into the mold of someone else, the outcomes will be substandard. Nobody pays to see the predictable; they pay to see the intriguing. By definition, your actual self is enticing. People will remember the thing you did that only you can do, not the thing you did that everyone can do.

Authenticity is in great demand in a society where conformity is the easy choice. Everyone wants to be more authentic, but we're all frightened of being the first. When you start living as your actual self, quirks and all, you offer others permission to do the same. We may not say it out, but everyone wants to see your authentic self. We yearn for authenticity.

Every good artistic breakthrough – artistic, musical, scientific, etc.

– is strange by definition because it provides a solution that is outside of the established paradigm. it necessitates a shift in thinking. Embracing your oddness provides you with a fresh viewpoint, and the world desperately needs a new perspective. The status quo does not foster innovation. When outsiders challenge the established quo with unusual ideas, this is when innovation occurs.

Everyone has their own qualities. Allowing ourselves to display these distinct features makes us happy. However, suppressing our distinctive features and denying our natural selves makes us feel bad and darkens our identities. Resistance to our distinctive features, however strange, results in a dark and inverted projection of self, much as a black hole emerges from the absence of a star.

Many individuals who conform do so because they are afraid of being alone. Standing out, on the other hand, will not make you lonely - far from it. By living honestly, you will meet others who share your oddness. This is your clan. When you step up and live your mission, you will discover those who have gone before you, and you will be an inspiration to those who will come after you.

On the surface, new notions, such as biological mutations, seem to be out of place. However, biological mutations, like new ideas, evolve through time and serve unexpected purposes. The mutation is eventually reproduced and contributes to the evolution of the species. Ideas are the evolutionary force that propels civilization forward. What is strange now may not be understood tomorrow, but it may become the new normal.

Others will perceive you as competent if you consider yourself as capable. Others will perceive you as incapable if you see yourself as unable. Self-perception has a lot of clout. It might be unsettling at first to stop fitting in and start sticking out. However, if you accept responsibility for your activities and disregard your fear of criticism, the world will conform to your vision of yourself to the extent of your conviction.

Embrace YOU

If you just remember one thing from this book, make it this: being a quirky oddball is a hidden benefit.

People fall in love with your eccentricities rather than your sameness, and they frequently don't recognize it. Your eccentricity serves as a differentiation. It's what piques people's interest and makes them want to learn more about you.

Your oddness is what jolts folks out of their smartphone-induced stupor and causes them to consider asking a question.

When there are a hundred job applications in front of you, your oddness will help you stand out.

Strangeness helps you create a connection with someone who has done great things and is tired of people asking for pictures with them instead of having a talk about weirdness that they will remember for the rest of their lives.

Strangeness draws together two persons who seem to have nothing in common. It's the "who the hell is that dude?" query that alters your life and reveals numerous previously unattainable options.

When you embrace it and begin to believe in your abilities, things start to become strange.

When people are motivated by your cause, you have achieved your goal. That's when you discover those individuals, that audience, who embrace you for who you really are, not because you're odd or unusual. You open the door to the possibility of shared humanity and enable others to see their own struggles mirrored in yours. Finally, you hear that lovely refrain: "Oh, you're strange? "I assumed I was the only one!" This is how companies are founded. This is how relationships develop. This is how you discover the right folks.

Embrace Your Weirdness

Things that made you strange as a child now make you brilliant. Accepting one's strangeness is a difficult personal decision, but it is, quite honestly, fascinating and fulfilling. We do it not for the sake of gain or achievement, but for our own freedom and to pave the road for others.

Being different is being powerful. Once you accept who you are, you will find that there are so many things to celebrate about you and so many ways in which it makes you more capable and impressive.

You can be a better worker, a better friend, a better lover and person if you accept the quirky, different parts of you that others might consider "weird."

Weird people make good lives - and they make history too.

Who Wants to be Normal?

Who Wants To Be Normal?

We all have peculiarities. Regardless of your background, personality, or even how visible you are in the eyes of the public, it is indisputable that we all do things that others may find strange. Yet, there are occasions when a prominent individual displays a personal eccentricity that perplexes the audience.

Sometimes these are minor eccentricities that the celebrity has become used to over time, and other times they are habits they developed as a result of commitment, superstition, or in their pursuit of success or beauty. In any case, these nuggets never fail to pique our attention, and it is that curiosity that led us to find these fascinating habits that some of the world's most famous people have.

The truth is that no one wants to be normal and some people have become major role models and huge successes by embracing that uniqueness that makes them, them.

How about Salvador Dali? When one thinks about surrealism, one is likely to think of Dali and his pomade-covered mustache. His life was as bizarre as his paintings, but apart from driving around in a vehicle full of cauliflowers and roaming around Paris with an anteater, there was something even stranger.

He treated Gala, his muse and love of his life, like a goddess when they married. He purchased her a castle and was only permitted to see his wife with a signed invitation.

Lev Tolstoy, the Russian literary great, not only authored historically correct works, but he also became historically significant while still living - and completely embracing his very unique personality.

Despite hailing from the highest level of society, Tolstoy ultimately began to doubt the morals of society in which he lived and began to take his own way.

He became a vegetarian, began a rigorous daily practice, and ridiculed the appearance of a wealthy man. He began wearing peasant clothing and shoes that he had manufactured himself, despite his lack of talent.

Throughout history, there have been countless people who have changed the world by not shying away from what made them unique, different, and totally themselves. These people survived and thrived not just because of their talent. They survived and thrived because they embraced a side of themselves that fostered their talent and really let it shine.

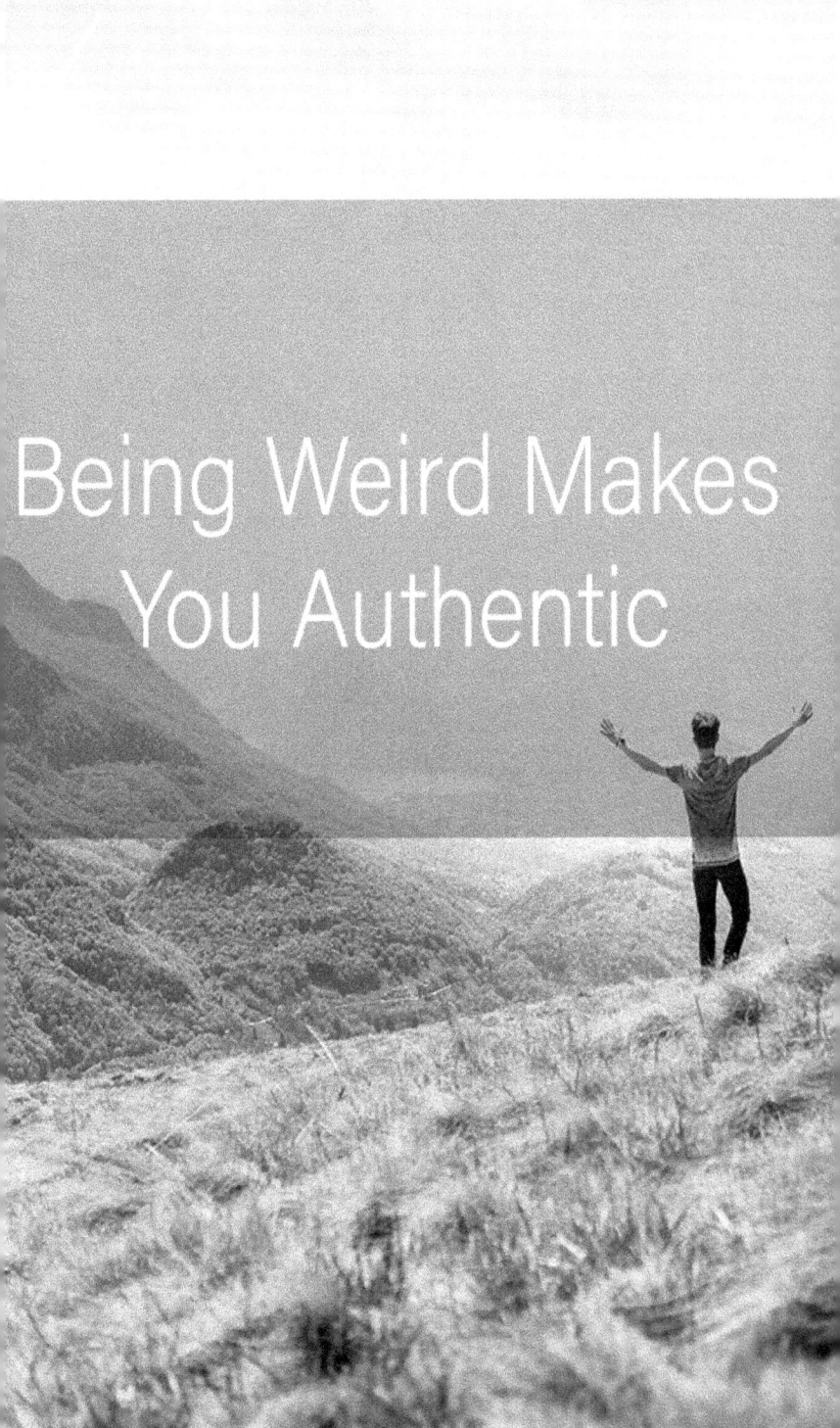

Being Weird Makes You Authentic

Weirdness is a positive thing. It distinguishes us and enables us to be completely different from the rest of the world while being fundamentally the very same. We Humans have a tendency to overlook that what makes us unique are the things we are passionate about, as well as the depths to which that enthusiasm might go.

We forget that such interests, whether they be reading books, playing Scrabble, or writing comic books, are valid and fantastic.

Imitation is how people learn to accomplish things. We have always done so and will continue to do so. It's the most certain approach to enhance your technique and understand the ins and outs of everything. Many people imitate those they admire when they are creating a personality of their own.

But the trouble with this is that we also discover who we are. And we learn to be someone other than ourselves. We look at the successful individuals, those who followed the rules, and we begin to chop away the portions of our life that don't fit. We lose our unique character quirks and personality, slowly but surely.

Then we wonder whether we can still listen to polka music or create rock operas if we want to be star workers and earn money. Or, if we really want to succeed in a creative profession, we must integrate our work into the mainstream.

We can't be anything other than the image of an employee, entrepreneur, or creative with whom people want to work.

We either consciously or unconsciously repeat this to ourselves, and we begin to feel embarrassed or ashamed of the way we were before we put ourselves into a nasty little box.

It wasn't like that when you were a youngster. You used to let your freak flag fly when you were a youngster. You rushed about in pink storm trooper gear, completely embracing everything about yourself.

But as you get older, you learn to tuck that side away, to find a place to lock it away so you can forget it was ever there.

Being Unique Makes You Creative

You'll never be able to embrace creativity if you try to run in lockstep with what you perceive to be the mainstream, with the worker in the cubicle next to you who always says and does the correct thing — rather than the real thing.

The finest solutions, ideas, and products do not emerge from traditional thinking. Some people may call this kind of thinking weird, but in reality, it's just unique, authentic, and can make you a stronger performer in all walks of life.

The ideas that come from being unique are the result of a creative twist that only a completely devoted freak could have devised. That is what you must strive towards. If you put a stop to it, you'll be suffocating whatever opportunity you had to be unique.

If you attempt to transform yourself into a stranger, someone you don't actually recognize when you look in the mirror and see grey where there used to be brilliant color, you'll end up hurting yourself sooner or later. It's going to smash you.

You'll begin to lose any sense of worth in your life, and you won't feel at ease in your own skin.

That is not the way to live. It's not the way to be. It's not a viable way to live. When you begin to lose the elements of yourself that give you a desire for life, that fire will eventually die out.

You Lose a Lot When You're Not Authentic

People will react when you aren't attempting to conceal your true nature. When you're exhibiting authenticity rather than a phony character, that's when you'll be able to reach out and connect with other people.

Allowing the world to see the genuine person underneath your skin rather than the image you wish to create.

Everything we accomplish represents a distinct aspect of our personality. But every portion is always based on something true, something that comes from me.

People you genuinely admire are well aware of their pursuits. This is a proven truth. Every creative is a passionate freak, whether they are entrepreneurs and founders, comic book artists, or speed metal bands. If they weren't, the world would be a far more colorful place.

Benjamin Franklin, Michael Bloomberg, Steve Jobs, Robin Williams, and Gertrude Stein are all motivated, authentic, and - to some - weird individuals. And it was those unique and authentic personalities that motivated them to accomplish things that have had an impact on millions, if not billions, of people.

You don't have to be a full-time artist or a founder. But it would be foolish to dismiss their successes and the things they were able to accomplish as a result of their interests. It's an indication that adhering to and sustaining yours is a worthwhile investment.

We want to celebrate our personality traits not just because it fosters authenticity, but also because when we work and live from our actual selves, we build a richer, stronger, more dynamic, and varied environment around us. This entails adding the distinct flavor of our particular abilities, character, and values to our job. It involves giving them the freedom to be themselves in your presence. It entails the world being a more true mirror of who we are, rather than who we believe we should be.

So, hold a mirror up to every beautiful part of your strangeness. Reconnect with your whole self and allow us to see every abstract, weirdly shaped, metallic rainbow component of it.

Think Outside the Box With Your Weirdness

Think Outside The Box With Your Weirdness

It's a fact that people who think outside the box and embrace being different get stuff done. They develop disruptive businesses, new technology, movements, and push others to think differently. All of our generation's incredible advances would not exist if weirdos did not exist to question the status quo.

How can we unleash our inner oddball in order to realize our full creative potential? And what can we do to be a bit weirder, a little better at thinking outside the box, and a little less tuned in to societal and cultural expectations? Because the answers to these questions demonstrate that being a bit odder may help us all become a lot more creative.

The normal individual will react to circumstances rapidly depending on the instructions given by those in charge. A distinctive or "weird" individual, on the other hand, is less inclined to heed authority or grasp social norms. Creative individuals live in a more hazy, fluid, ethereal environment, and although a highly original person may seem unusual or peculiar to others, it is precisely this sort of social oddity that leads to creative breakthroughs.

People who are open to new experiences and have the capacity to challenge the current quo might interpret their surroundings in novel ways. Looking for the unexpected and venturing outside of your own experience leads to creativity. Being strange to some is just being open to new experiences and ideas.

Always Try New Things

But how do you open yourself up even more and push your creative and think-outside-the-box mentality? Simple, you practice what you preach.

It has long been questioned whether creativity can be taught, yet it is commonly agreed that being open to new experiences is a creative attribute that can be taught. There's no excuse if all you need to be more creative is to go out of your comfort zone!

Patronize a different ethnic restaurant, learn a language, do the hardest crossword puzzle you can find, read a tough book - any experience, as long as it's new and beyond your comfort zone, can broaden your thinking and make you more creative. Some may label you as odd, but genuinely creative individuals understand that being open to new experiences and trying new things is one of the greatest ways to create fresh, unique connections and generate creative ideas.

Remember Your Story is Different

Each of us has expereinced a unique combination of events that have shaped us into the people we are today. People from unusual origins, on the other hand, tend to be the most creative since they have a distinct view of the world.

Surprise occurrences and unusual experiences might range from living overseas to having a tragedy in the family, and they all provide what psychologists call "cognitive flexibility," which boosts creativity.

In some ways, we all come from strange backgrounds. Nobody was raised the same way we were. And no one else sees the world the same way we do. Although it may seem overwhelming to comprehend how much some individuals have gone through, everyone has gone through, done, imagined, or felt something completely unique – something which no one else has ever gone through. That's quite incredible. As a result, some individuals are able to be creative because of their ability to harness their background and the distinct viewpoint it has given them.

The secret to unlocking your innermost creativity is to reflect and get to the core of what makes you unique. Finding out what makes you unique might be challenging, but once you discover it, you have a clear road to creativity because all you have to do is perceive the world through your unique perspective, which is as simple as being yourself.

So, how do you discover what makes you unique? Try identifying yourself by asking yourself questions such as, "What am I particularly good at?" "What are my favorite things?" "What do I find appealing?" "What do I find repulsive?" "How would my friends characterize me?" "How would I characterize myself?" "What would I do if

I had an hour to myself?" Have a free day? A month off? A year off? These kinds of inquiries go deep into what makes you tick and what your priorities are.

By getting to know yourself better, you'll be able to figure out what kind of craziness you can bring to the table, whether in a group or on your own. Although some individuals come from more unusual backgrounds than others, we all have a unique set of experiences that no one else has. We all have our own unique perspectives on the world, and we all have the power to communicate them. Being unique, therefore, is a matter of perspective. We're all different.

The distinction in our creative potential is how much we've been able to capitalize on our own brand of weirdness.

Tap Your Weirdness Potential

Understanding what it means to be strange is accepting that we all have the capacity for oddness. And, although this isn't always a compliment, it most certainly is when it comes to innovation.

Strange individuals are trailblazers. A crazy person's brain does not exclude ideas just because they do not seem to be absolutely vital at the moment. I may not have been able to write this piece if Steve Jobs had done that.

Everything we go through, no matter how typical or strange our lives seem to be, is fuel for future creation and should therefore be stored, unpacked, and tinkered with until all of these concepts combine into fresh, creative ideas. Keeping an open mind to new experiences is a terrific approach to add to your creative arsenal. Another approach is to recognize your distinct point of view on the world. And, although collective thinking may be detrimental to creativity, the capacity to seek out other odd people is one of the most effective methods to generate new ideas. So go out there and proudly wear your odd badge. Besides, why would you want to be normal when it's the oddballs that have the power to alter the world?

Embracing Your Weird Makes You Mentally Strong

Embracing Your Weird Makes You Mentally Strong

Being honest to yourself is one of the most self-loving things you can do. You should feel proud if someone tells you that you're strange.

To be yourself, you must first understand yourself. You know what brings you joy and what your point of view is. Because you know yourself, you make excellent decisions.

Perhaps you can ride a horse, play a musical instrument, speak a couple of languages, or draw really well. Perhaps you've been to other nations and experienced diverse cultures. Because you are not scared to try anything out of the ordinary, you have accomplished much and would want to learn more!

Some individuals are afraid to walk to a grocery store alone because they believe everyone is judging them, but that is not the case with you. Some individuals can't even register for courses without the help of their buddies, but that's not you; you take anything you want. Keep up the good work!

Why would you say anything about others if you don't care what others think of you? You are tolerant and open-minded because you have to be in order to embrace yourself.

It's true. Haters will always hate. Not everyone shares your sense of style. If you believe you're wonderful, you probably are!

Your friends trust you and enjoy how much fun you are since you are always yourself, honest, and not shady.

Because you will not allow anybody to pull you down, you have control over how you feel. You are one of the most powerful people you know. And you will only feel more mentally strong when you truly embrace who you are and why you are. Don't be afraid of your personality, your quirks, or your unique nature. In fact, you need to look at it as your weapon, a tool to make yourself more confident and sure that you really are unlike anyone else- and that's a good thing.

Weirdness Makes You Irreplaceable: The Unfair Advantage of Being Weird

Hopefully, by now you have accepted the fact that you're a bit different from other people. You know that you're not like everyone else and you never will be. As stated before, that should be embraced. You should lean into it.

However, you should never forget that being your true authentic, unusual self has a lot of advantages that more "normal" and traditional people just don't have. These features come in hand at work, at home, and anywhere in the world. These advantages set you up for more success. You just have to be aware of them and ready to use them at your disposal.

What are the advantages of being a bit kooky and odd? If you're what some people consider "werid" you have probably noticed the following about yourself.

You Aren't Afraid of Speaking Your Mind

We live in a world where people are too afraid to say what they really think and feel. People are scared of rocking the boat, sure that it will lead to being fired or losing friends or just being cast aside and being declared an outsider.

But people who embrace their oddness also embrace how they feel and aren't afraid to say so. Let's be honest, that's usually the best approach for any situation. You should always speak your truth and say what's bothering you, no matter if it's polite or not.

You should never hide your feelings.

Saying the truth about what you feel can sometimes lead to some amazing things. Think of all the businesses that wouldn't have gotten off the ground if people weren't daring enough and didn't say what they really thought. Think of all the risks that wouldn't have been taken. Speaking your mind is the first step to making real change and real change is necessary if you want honest success.

Therefore, if you are someone who is comfortable in your skin and comfortable being odd, you are comfortable making changes and making waves and, yes, rocking the boat. But that's a good thing.

You Are Comfortable in Your Own Skin

Being comfortable in your own skin is the only way you can truly get ahead in the world. It allows you to have confidence in yourself and confident people are willing to try harder.

Confident people who are comfortable in their skin and okay with who they are and what they look and act like are more likely to try for a job promotion or ask someone on a date or embrace an art project they have always wanted to tackle. You can't really think you're worthy of great things - and fight for them - unless you feel good about yourself and are comfortable in your skin.

People who are often considered weird are more likely to be okay with who they are. In fact, they don't seem to care what other people think. They have cultivated a personality that doesn't bother with the thoughts of others and they do their own thing and follow the beat of their own drum. That's a great thing and leads to true belief in themselves and true accomplishments because of that.

You Are Creative

Creative people make the world go round. While the world needs plenty of lawyers and doctors and construction workers, it also needs art and creative endeavors. Without them, the world just feels much more flat and empty.

Creative people are more often than not considered a bit odd or different. Their personalities are a bit more eccentric and over the top. And this sort of personality usually leads to better art and better creative projects.

And why are creative people usually "weird"? From the first drop of paint on the canvas to the art show, the creative process encompasses a variety of emotions, desires, talents, and behaviors. It would be astonishing if these feelings, qualities, and actions didn't often clash throughout the creative process, causing inner and outside friction. Indeed, creative individuals are often seen as strange, quirky, and eccentric.

Scientists have sought to capture the characteristics of creative individuals throughout the years. But putting them under the microscope hasn't been simple. According to psychologists, creative persons show tendencies of thought and action that are segregated in most people. They comprise opposing extremes. And they need those extremes to be creative.

There are several phases to creativity. Those who are capable of achieving the pinnacles of human creative expression possess all of these features and behaviors inside themselves and are able to flip back and forth between them depending on the stage of the creative process and what is most adaptable at the time.

You Are Mentally Strong

What are the most important skills we should instill in today's children?

There are various types, but mental strength is the one that will definitely help them develop into their best selves and overcome life's most difficult problems.

Mental strength needs paying attention to three things: how you think, feel, and behave. Thinking large, feeling well, and behaving bravely all contribute to the development of our mental muscles.

Of course, getting to the point where you'll perform these things automatically requires practice, patience, and continual reinforcement. People who are distinct, unique, and strange seem to be considerably more intellectually powerful.

One of the main reasons for this is that these individuals are conscious of their emotions. They are aware of how they behave and think. They have a greater understanding of themselves, their inner workings, and the way their thoughts function - even if others don't.

Here are some of the reasons why odd people are mentally stronger than others.

They Say No

Everyone struggles from time to time to stand out, say no, or voice their views. However, depending on the circumstances, refusing to answer yes might make you stronger.

Many individuals find it difficult to say no because it feels uncomfortable and strange. However, by mustering the guts to do it more often, they will discover that it becomes simpler with time. It also alleviates the tension of being forced to do things they don't want to do. Those that are seen as unusual are typically pretty comfortable with the idea of declaring they don't want to do anything. They aren't scared of upsetting the status quo or coming out as arrogant, so if they don't want to do anything, they'll simply say so. This results in increased mental power, stability, and comfort.

They're Adaptable

Change is difficult, whether it's a new job, school, or location. It's normal to miss the way things used to be or to be concerned that what's going on will make things worse.

But mentally healthy individuals realize that, even if it doesn't seem like it at first, change may help them develop into a stronger person.

Sadly, most of us do not devote enough time to contemplating our emotions. In reality, we often use more energy battling our feelings.

People with unusual personalities, on the other hand, may go with the flow. They keep their cool, roll with the punches, and find ways to land on their feet. When you look at the world through a new, unusual lens, you are less fearful of things being upended and the status quo altering. This provides a lot more peace of mind, particularly when things become difficult.

They Believe in Themselves

People who feel empowered do not rely on others to make them happy. They may choose to appear cheerful even while others are having a terrible day or want to vent their rage on them.

This will assist to drown out the negative voices in their heads that attempt to tell them they don't have what it takes to achieve. The best catchphrases are brief and simple to remember:

Belief in oneself may make or break a person's life. It's the ideal approach to go ahead, attain your goals and objectives, and, most importantly, have fun while doing it.

It's not always simple to believe in oneself. It's difficult to silence the negative voices in our thoughts that we all hear. Unique and strange individuals, on the other hand,

Embrace Your Weirdness

have spent their whole lives disregarding the people and beliefs that oppose them. As a result, they've been cheering themselves on for years and empowering themselves at every step.

People who are labeled "strange" by others are more inclined to trust in themselves and help drive themselves through the finish line.

Get Noticed for Your Weirdness

Get Noticed For Your Weirdness: How To Embrace Your Weirdness

Perhaps you feel different but not different enough. Maybe you feel like you are holding back some of the things that make you so unique. Maybe you're not feeling like you're reaching your full potential of personality.

Now that you know that people who others call strange are the ones most likely to be comfortable, happy, and successful, you might be asking how you can reach new heights in strangeness. Here are a few tips to follow if you want to be the realest you possible.

Create New Skills

Make yourself useful in any setting to ensure that other people find you fascinating. Many social scientists and professionals advise you to take on or strive to acquire as many valuable talents as possible, ranging from web design to vehicle repair.

That way, whether a buddy needs a website for her new company or a blanket for her infant niece, you'll always be the go-to guy.

Stay Curious

One method to guarantee that you're uninteresting is to close yourself off to opposing thoughts and points of view. Instead, actively seek out fresh ideas and experiences that will alter your thinking and feelings.

Keep an open mind and be inquisitive. Allow for a complicated world with many interpretations. Learn new things to widen and develop your viewpoint. Be a lifelong learner. Learning does not stop after you graduate from high school. There is always something fresh to learn about and immerse oneself in.

Follow Your Passions

Instead of studying about a bunch of boring things merely to be educated, focus on areas that you find interesting. When you describe them to others, you'll sound more energetic and engaging.

Life is too short to not follow your passion and embrace what you love. One of the benefits of doing that is that you're happier. It also happens to make you successful too.

It's not so much a question of attempting to be intriguing as it is of simply pursuing your interests, of being an ardent student and collector of knowledge that intrigues and thrills you.

Read - A LOT

When you have the time and money to explore the globe, that's fantastic. Even if you don't, you can learn about many cultures and historical times by reading whatever you can get your hands on.

Books, blogs, and journals – read as many fresh tales and ideas as you can.

According to studies, those who read more fiction are more empathetic and understanding of others. Those are two qualities and personality characteristics that everyone should aspire towards. People that read a lot may be labeled as nerds or "weird" but if they're creating such wonderful, strong, and comfortable personalities, it doesn't matter what others think of them.

Be Unconventional

Being intriguing boils down to being distinct from everyone else.

However, not everyone has the money or the willingness to deviate from the road and pursue their every whim. Consider the strange events you've previously experienced. Maybe you've lived in another country, you can recite poetry from memory, you're good at impressions, and you can fit your fist in your mouth. The possibilities are endless. There's bound to be something, so keep looking for that aspect of yourself that no one else has.

Being Weird in the Office

Being Weird In The Office

Here's something you probably never thought of: being different, odd, or weird can actually be a huge benefit when you're working with other people.

For years, people have thought they needed to be "normal" and on their best behavior at work. No one wants to feel like an outcast or apart from the crowd. But the truth is that being different is actually something you can use to your advantage, no matter where you work. Why? What is it about being odd that can be such a huge tool that will advance your career and help you be the best worker you can be?

First and foremost, "weird" should not imply encouraging unproductive conduct or oddity for the sake of weirdness. It entails persuading workers to divulge their quirks and interests, the things that make them unique. Revelations may be a powerful tool for team development. When people speak about things you wouldn't typically talk about because you'd be ashamed, they turn up on the first day and there's already an intimacy.

Weirdness at work fosters innovation by allowing individuals to express themselves and provide unique ideas. Strange, on the other hand, comes in a variety of shapes. Some of the most bright and creative individuals are often the most prickly and nasty. A little oddness makes you feel warm and cozy. However, the type of quirkiness that, in theory, leads to innovation and transformation is also what makes us uncomfortable.

In that spirit, it's critical for any company to have a few distinctive, strange, and one-of-a-kind employees to question the current quo. It will keep the firm reaching for more, experimenting with new ideas, and breaking the mold. There isn't a successful company that hasn't sought to shake things up in some manner. People who are unusual, if not peculiar, are frequently at the foundation of this. Quirky individuals prefer to attempt new things, and new things may lead to huge success in business.

"Weird" describes both the culture and the workforce: it is a synonym for genuine, laidback, and amusing. The amount of strangeness that a firm can accept depends on the industry. If you work in a hotel or restaurant, you want employees with large personalities, but you also need people who can provide excellent customer service and empathy.

People may grow even wilder and really lean into their anti-social yet great personality qualities in other businesses that don't depend on face-to-face interactions with customers. People in these occupations may be as strange as they choose to be.

Yes, conventional wisdom holds that office-politicking extroverts are the most suited for success. As a consequence, if you're eccentric, you've undoubtedly believed that the aspects of your personality that look out of sync are flaws that must be addressed.

However, as we have seen, this argument is faulty and false. What businesses really need are enthusiastic, innovative minds. Businesses need "disruptors," as well as people who are too eccentric to grasp how things are "supposed to work." Do not be afraid of being who you really are. You do not need to alter your essential being in order to flourish in your work. When in doubt, keep the following in mind:

- Your distinct point of view is a source of strength, not weakness.

- Sensitivity is what enables you to read and, presumably, play to a room.

- Because of your emotional intensity and personality and outsider position, you're not always attempting to court favor with an uninteresting employer or phony coworkers.

And here are some reasons why being different or odd could make your business a huge hit. Remember, other people will notice the difference in your personality and many of them will be drawn to it.

Being Normal is Boring

Scarcity raises the value. Diamonds are valued largely due to their scarcity. Sand and salt are significantly less valuable, not because they are unusable, but because they are so common and abundant.

Being Different Makes You Noticeable

We become invisible when we blend in and follow the crowd. No one can see us if we execute our jobs correctly. Everyone drives right by if our company fits in. Nobody comes to a halt. They have no idea we're even there. If they do stop, they don't stay long and don't purchase anything since our products or services are the same as everyone else's. We don't get noticed if we fit in. And

one of the most significant things we can get from consumers is their attention.

Being Odd is Surprising - and Exciting

Surprises have a higher chance of persuading consumers. We may elicit an emotional reaction by surprising someone. As part of an emotional reaction, our brain is structured to release dopamine. Surprising and eventually pleasing a consumer creates a long-lasting impact and can also create life-long customers.

Being Unique Makes You Memorable

We recall the extraordinary experiences in our life rather than the routine ones. If no one recalls your brand message, you won't be able to impact them. One of the compliments you can get is that you are different and, therefore, memorable. We remember unusual individuals and companies.

Being Normal is Easy to Imitate

When there exist viable alternatives, the value of any product or service quickly declines. A clear illustration comes from the workplace. When a machine or an outsourced contractor in another place can perform someone's work quicker or cheaper, that person's employment becomes less valuable. The compensation for that post falls, as does the chance of being replaced.

Imitation is avoided by original brands. They make it tough to replace them. There are no suitable replacements.

Having the confidence to celebrate your differences and express your thoughts can help you thrive in almost any profession. So keep going. Encourage yourself to offer thoughts or solutions to long-standing issues. Make a proposal for your huge, crazy fantasy project. Embrace your oddness; it's more valuable than you realize.

Never Be Forgotten by Embracing Your Weirdness

Never Be Forgotten By Embracing Your Weirdness

When you truly embrace your differences from other people and accept who you are and how you are, you will not only become more comfortable in your skin, you will become more memorable to other people.

In fact, when you think back on the people who had the biggest impact on your life, it's likely that at least a few of them were a bit odd, to put it gently. Perhaps it was a student you studied with who was very quirky, maybe it was a co-worker or friend who did things their own way. In the end, you'll remember these people more than anyone else. Not because of the kooky things they did, but because of the personality they had and the way they carried and believed in themselves.

Being different will make you memorable. It will prevent you from ever being forgotten. If you really want to leave a mark in someone's mind, you need to wholly accept the odd, peculiar nature that makes you you.

Why? Why are different or odd people so darn memorable? What makes them leave such a lasting impression on us?

They're Never Boring

You have to admit that "odd" people just do things differently. They're never going to bore you, that's for sure. They have their own quirks, their own styles, and their own opinions that feel completely valid, natural, and authentic.

You never really know what you're going to get with an odd person. You never know how they might surprise you. That is exciting and, generally, way more enjoyable to be around than a traditional and rather boring person.

They Always Reveal New Things

When you start dating someone, you are not dealing with a genuine person. People begin a relationship by displaying a version of themselves, then gradually peel back the layers until the true person is exposed.

If you're dating an eccentric, you'll always be discovering new and different and exciting things. Perhaps two months into the relationship, they disclose that they know the first hundred digits of pi. Then, a year later, you discover they've watched every single episode of Star Trek or speak Pig Latin well.

You'll have to stay around to discover about such things. And each time you do, it's like a prize that will make a lasting effect on someone.

They Teach You About Yourself

Most of us go through life with a lot of preconceived notions about ourselves. When you spend time with unusual people, you learn how you actually feel about things. It's the foundation for the vast majority of rom-coms, and there's a reason for that.

You realize how judgmental you are. It's simple to let people live their life any way they want, but it's a different story when you care about the individual. They will teach you about yourself and about how you see others and treat others too. It will be a way to build yourself into the type of person you want to be.

They Teach you that No One is Normal

Perhaps the biggest impact strange people can have on others is when they teach you that no one is really normal. No one is totally, 100% traditional. Everyone has quirks. Everyone is different. Everyone has something inside of them that sets them apart, even if they try to hide it.

The world would be a better place if more people accepted who they were, quirks and all. When you look back on your life, you will see the odd people that came in and out of it and remember that they made you comfortable to be your authentic self and they taught you that everyone is strange in their own ways. Is there any better gift than that?

Conclusion

Conclusion

If you have learned anything here, hopefully, it's that oddness is good. Whatever you want to call it - weirdness, uniqueness, peculiarity, being distinct and different - it is something that should be celebrated and accepted and embraced by everyone.

It's great to be unique. It's also bankable.

Do you know someone who is one-of-a-kind or perhaps odd? Astronauts. Saints. Nobel Prize laureates. Winners are odd. Success stories are filled with unique people. People who have never heard of or are hesitant to attempt new interests. People who are not afraid to voice their thoughts. People who are both problem solvers and solution seekers. People who are not similar to you. Being strange entails being clearly different. It refers to being or doing anything that causes others to look, laugh, applaud, or boo. And it's something we should all strive towards.

In the world of business or your own personal life, being unique and completely your own self can get you far. You can find great success by dancing to the beat of your own drum and casting aside worries about what other people will think of you.

When you are comfortable in your own skin and sure of who you are and why you are and the sort of personality and quirks you have, you will feel strong and capable of so much. You will believe in yourself and that will affect other people. It will help fire them up, help lead them, and it will leave a long-lasting, undeniable impact on them too.

It's the strange people and the ones with the most quirks who really touch us the most. These are the ones we are drawn to, the ones we can't look away from, the ones we want to support and follow.

People who are afraid of being themselves and afraid of rocking the boat rarely get far. They don't believe they can do more than the average person, they don't think they should open their mouths and stand up or fight for themselves. They want to be part of the crowd that follows, not the pack that leads.

When you embrace what makes you different, you show others what you have to offer. Not only that, you make life so much easier. You can feel at home in your own mind and your body.

You can believe in yourself and not really worry about what others think or feel.

Loving yourself and believing in yourself is important. You can't get anywhere until you master that. Let your freak flag fly. Believe in yourself. Know that you have something vital and important to offer. Because you do. You really do.

This is a sample text.

www.ingramcontent.com/pod-product-compliance
Lightning Source LLC
LaVergne TN
LVHW061602070526
838199LV00077B/7147